Praise for Trevor Paglén and I COULD TELL YOU.

"A fascinating set of shoulder patches designed for the [ ] Ops programs." —Stephen Colbert, *The Colbert Re[port]*

"A glimpse of [the Pentagon's] dark world through a revealing lens— patches—the kind worn on military uniforms...The book offers not only clues into the nature of the secret programs, but also a glimpse of zealous male bonding among the presumed elite of the military-industrial complex. The patches often feel like fraternity pranks gone ballistic." —William Broad, *The New York Times*

"A fresh approach to secret government. It shows that these secret programs have their own culture, vocabulary and even sense of humor." —Steven Aftergood, The Federation of American Scientists

"Gives readers a peek into the shadows...Department of Defense spokesman Bob Mehal told *Newsweek* that it 'would not be prudent to comment on what patches did or did not represent classified units.' That's OK. Some mysteries are more fun when they stay unsolved." —Karen Pinchin, *Newsweek*

"An impressive collection." —Justin Rood, ABC News

"An art book that presents peculiar shoulder patches created for the weird and top secret programs funded by the Pentagon's black budget... an achievement." —Timothy Buckwalter, *San Francisco Chronicle*

"I was fascinated...[Paglen] has assembled about 40 colorful patch insignia from secret, military 'black' programs that are hardly ever discussed in public. He has plenty of regalia from the real denizens of Area 51." —Alex Beam, *The Boston Globe*

"Some of the worst crimes in the American landscape are hiding in plain sight, and nobody has ever pursued them more thoroughly or explained them more chillingly and engagingly than Trevor Paglen. What he is doing is important, fascinating, and groundbreaking."
—Rebecca Solnit, author of *Wanderlust*

"The iconography of the United States military. Not the mainstream military, with its bars and ribbons and medals, but the secret or 'black projects' world, which may or may not involve contacting aliens, building undetectable spy aircraft, and experimenting with explosives that could make atomic bombs look like firecrackers. Here, mysterious characters and cryptic symbols hint at intrigue much deeper than rank, company, and unit." —*UTNE Reader*

"Of course, issuing patches for a covert operation sounds like a joke...but truth be told, these days everything is branded. Military symbols are frequently replete with heraldic imagery—some rooted in history, others based on contemporary popular arts that feature comic characters—but these enigmatic dark-op images, in some cases probably designed by the participants themselves, are more personal, and also more disturbing, than most."
—Steven Heller, *The New York Times Book Review*

"Trevor Paglen gets into the black heart of America's black sites. There is no better guide to this great American mystery. What goes on inside these bases will determine the future of warfare—and who we are—for the rest of the century." —Robert Baer, former case officer at the CIA and author of *See No Evil: The True Story of a Ground Soldier in the CIA's War on Terrorism*

I COULD TELL YOU
BUT THEN YOU WOULD HAVE TO
BE DESTROYED BY ME

EMBLEMS FROM THE PENTAGON'S BLACK WORLD

TREVOR PAGLEN

MELVILLE HOUSE PUBLISHING

BROOKLYN, NEW YORK

INTRODUCTION

I began taking patches and military iconography seriously a number of years ago while visiting California's Antelope Valley in the westernmost region of the Mojave Desert. The Antelope Valley is the nerve center of the United States' military aviation industry and home to the Air Force Flight Test Center at Edwards Air Force Base. Made famous by the film *The Right Stuff*, Edwards is where Chuck Yeager broke the sound barrier in 1947, where Pete Knight pushed the experimental X-15 rocket plane towards Mach 7 twenty years later, and where the space shuttle *Columbia* landed after its first space flight in 1981. The Flight Test Center's motto *Ad Inexplorata* (Into the Unknown) speaks to the history of experimental aviation research that defines the region. On that particular day, I was visiting Peter Merlin, an "aerospace archaeologist" with a penchant for tracking down historic aircraft crash sites and a knowledgeable researcher of military aviation history. One of Merlin's particular areas of expertise is the history of "black" (i.e. secret) aviation projects, which is why I had traveled to the Antelope Valley to meet him.

As we sat in his living room, Merlin told me about the history of what people in defense circles call the "black world" of classified projects, and recounted stories of the brief glimpses he'd seen of it. He told me about the time he'd spent standing on a ridgeline in the middle of the Nevada desert looking down on the Air Force's secret base near Groom Lake. He told me rumors and

Opposite:
Boeing–McDonnell Douglas' "Bird of Prey" advanced technology demonstrator was first flown in 1996. Its existence was declassified in 2002.
Credit: USAF

anecdotes about a $300 million CIA-Air Force plane that never got off the ground, about a mysterious "classified demonstrator" flown in the mid 1980s, and about a secret plane called the YF-113G that flew in the early 1990s. The bits of arcana he had picked up in his work were as dizzying in their incompleteness as they were fascinating.

After spending the better part of an afternoon chatting, Merlin motioned for me to follow him upstairs and into his office. There, I found myself surrounded by the refuse, leftovers, and bits of debris that a half-century of secret aircraft projects had left behind. He'd recovered metal shards from shattered stealth fighters by locating the remote sites where they had crashed, and found the in-flight recorder from an A-12 spy plane in a local junkyard. There were mugs, pins, and other memorabilia preserved in frames, glass-enclosed shelves, and well-kept vitrines. "I trust evidence," Merlin said. "People can lie. Evidence doesn't." He handed me a thick folder stuffed with documents. "Here's the Standard Operating Procedure for Area 51," the operations manual for a secret Air Force Base, "most people just assume that everything is classified so they don't take the time to look," he said. Indeed, a few months later, I would obtain my own copy from the ever-helpful staff at the National Archives. "And this," he told me as he opened a notebook filled with scanned images of military patches, "is called 'patch intel.'"

I'd seen some of the images he had reproduced in his notebooks before, lining the walls of test pilot watering holes, on the living room walls of other people I'd talked to, and on the pages of in-house military history publications. They were a part of the military's everyday culture. I'd always found the skulls, lightning bolts, and dragons that adorned these patches to be fairly unremarkable, but Merlin saw something in them that I hadn't noticed—the symbols they contained were far from random. The lightning bolts, he told me, meant specific things in specific contexts; the numbers of stars on an image might represent a unit number or an operating location; the symbols on a patch could be clues to the purpose of a hidden program or a cover story designed to divert attention away from a program. These symbols, Merlin explained to me, were a language. If you could begin to learn its grammar, you could get a glimpse into the secret world itself.

And so I began to collect. When I toured interesting military bases, I took note of the symbols that its personnel wore. I started making sketches of interesting images I'd seen. As I amassed more interviews with military and intelligence-types, I always made a point of asking about patches or other memorabilia that they might have in their possession. If I saw something noteworthy adorning the wall of a bar or the home of a retired NCO, I would ask to take a photo. In many cases, people freely gave me a copy of what they had lying around. I began writing to Freedom of Information Act officers and base historians at different military installations, requesting images associated with obscure programs. Sometimes, this actually produced results. I began to amass more and more images and started to learn how to separate the diamonds from the rough. I had acquired a collector's obsession.

PATCHES

If we, rather arbitrarily, picked a date to begin the story of how patches and icons enveloped so much contemporary military culture, we might choose the summer of 1862.

That summer, so the story goes, the Army of the Potomac's Third Corps commander, General Philip Kearny, came across a group of Union officers lounging under a tree by the road side. Assuming that the wayward men were stragglers from his own command, Kearny, who was a strict disciplinarian, launched into an explosion of expletives and invectives directed at the officers. The men stood at attention, patiently waiting until the commander's vocal chords gave out. When Kearny finished, one of the men raised his hand and meekly suggested that Kearny had possibly made a mistake: the officers didn't belong in Kearny's brigade after all. Realizing his error, Kearny is said to have instantly turned into a model gentleman: "Pardon me; I will take steps to know how to recognize my own men hereafter." Kearny proceeded to order his men to place a piece of red cloth on the front of their caps, so that they might be distinguished from other officers. The enlisted men under his command followed.

The piece of red cloth became known as the "Kearny patch," and, with it, the modern system of unit insignias was born. In less than a year, Major General Joseph Hooker had ordered the entire eastern army to wear distinctive patches: the First Corps would wear a circle, the Second Corps a trefoil, the Eleventh Corps a crescent, and the Twelfth Corps a star.

As the war spread, so did the system of insignia. The patches began to take on special meanings. When the Twelfth Corps went to Chattanooga to aid the Fifteenth Corps, an Irish soldier from the latter division joined some of the newly-arrived men around the fire. Noticing that the men all wore stars on their uniforms, the Irishman asked if the men were all brigadier-generals. The men from the Twelfth replied that the star was their corps badge, and that everyone wore them. "What is your badge?" they asked. "Forty rounds in the cartridge box, and twenty in the pocket," the Irishman replied. Soon thereafter, the Fifteenth Corps adopted a cartridge box and forty rounds as its symbol.

The tradition of unit insignia has been with the military ever since. There are now thousands and thousands of patches in the modern armed forces, depicting everything from a soldier's unit,

to the many programs a soldier might be charged with, to his or her role within an organization. There are patches custom-made to commemorate special events, and "Friday" patches (informal, and often more colorful, patches that airmen are allowed to wear on Fridays). Simply put, the military has patches for almost everything it does. Including, curiously, for programs, units, and activities that are officially secret.

Above: The Civil War Era "Kearney Patch" represents one of the earliest American military patches. *Photo: T. Glen Larson*

THE BLACK WORLD

The easiest way to see the outlines of the Pentagon's black world is to download a copy of the defense budget from the Department of Defense Comptroller's web site. Buried in the RDT&E (Research Development, Test, and Evaluation) section is a very long list of peculiar line items:

PROGRAM ELEMENT #0603801F:	SPECIAL PROGRAMS	$317 MILLION
PROGRAM ELEMENT #0207248F:	SPECIAL EVALUATION PROGRAM	$530 MILLION
PROGRAM ELEMENT #0301324F:	FOREST GREEN	[NO NUMBER]
PROGRAM ELEMENT #0304111F:	SPECIAL ACTIVITIES	[NO NUMBER]
PROGRAM ELEMENT #0301555G:	CLASSIFIED PROGRAMS	[NO NUMBER]

And there are many, many more. These line items are an unclassified glimpse at the so-called "black budget," the annual expenditures for classified programs. To get a "best guess" estimate of the black budget's size, you can add up all the line items and compare that number to the budget's published total. If you do so, you'll notice a discrepancy. A big discrepancy—about $30 billion.

This black budget doesn't disappear into a vacuum—it is the lifeblood of the Pentagon's black world.

In defense jargon, the phrase "black world" denotes the collection of programs, people, and places involved in the most secret of military projects. Like the black budget, the black world is as vast as it is secret. It is not so much a world unto itself as it is a world existing alongside and interwoven with the more conventional parts of military and civilian life. Airbases such as Edwards Air Force Base in Southern California have restricted "compounds" where black projects take place. Industrial sites like Lockheed Martin's Skunk Works have cordoned off areas dedicated to classified projects. Deputy directors of various military agencies are charged with overseeing projects whose existence might be kept secret even from their commanders. Black operations are also woven into existing, visible, activities: like a classified payload aboard a rocket launch from Vandenberg Air Force Base. Or the 1990 space shuttle mission STS-36 (piloted by a former deputy chief of the Air Force's Special Projects Office), which is long rumored to have deployed a supersecret stealth satellite, code-named MISTY, before landing at Edwards Air Force Base.

The black world also has its dedicated bases, such as the Air Force's "operating location near Groom Lake," a Nevada aircraft test site popularly known as Area 51 where the "Special Projects Flight Test Squadron" tests classified airframes. To the north of Groom Lake is the Tonopah Test Range (also known as Area 52), where a squadron of purloined Soviet MiGs once flew, piloted by a unit called the "Red Eagles" under the code name CONSTANT PEG. During the 1980s, Tonopah was also home to operational squadrons of then-classified F-117a stealth fighters, and patches identified their wearers as "Grim Reapers," "Nightstalkers," and "Goat Suckers."

It's difficult to figure out what goes on behind the restricted airspaces, the closed doors, the cover stories, and the official denials of the Pentagon's black world. It's all secret. But from time to time, the black world peeks out into the "white" world, and those paying close attention can get a fleeting glimpse.

Military radio aficionado Steve Douglass got such a glimpse in early 2004 when his scanners recorded an aircraft using the call sign "Lockheed Test 2334" telling an Albuquerque air traffic controller that it would be "going supersonic somewhere above Flight Level 60 [60,000 feet]." When the controller asked for the aircraft type, the unnamed pilot responded that "We are classified type and cannot reveal our true altitude." A few minutes later, Douglass heard the mysterious aircraft ask for clearance to descend to 30,000 feet and a flight path toward "Las Vegas with final destination somewhere in the Nellis Range," the giant Nevada military range that is home to Groom Lake and the Tonopah Test Range. "Trip home a bit slower, eh?" said the controller.

Another glimpse had come the year before when U-2 pilots flying missions over Iraq (and possibly even more "sensitive" places) started complaining about mysterious high flying Unmanned Aerial Vehicles (UAVs) operating at the same extreme altitudes as their spy planes. Too close for comfort, in the pilots' collective opinion. When defense industry journalists picked up on the sightings, Pentagon officials seemed to confirm the classified aircraft's existence, explaining that the enigmatic aircraft bore a family resemblance to another Lockheed UAV nicknamed "DarkStar."

A search through the published biographies of Air Force test pilots reveals a different kind of peephole into the black world. In open records, we find men like Joseph Lanni, whose resumé says that he commanded a "classified flight test squadron" from 1995-1997, and flew "numerous classified prototypes," including something called the "YF-24."

And then, for a different kind of glimpse into the black world, there are the patches and symbols reproduced in this book.

WHY?

If the symbols and patches contained in this book refer to classified military programs, the existence of which is often a state secret, why do these patches exist in the first place? Why jeopardize the secrecy of these projects by attaching images to them at all—no matter how obscure or indirect those images might be? Why advertise the fact that someone might be involved in black projects, even with words like "I'd tell you but then I'd have to kill you," or "NOYFB" and the like? No doubt, the short answer is itself some sort of variation of "I'd tell you but I'd have to kill you."

We can speculate about the best answer, perhaps, by looking back to the history of unit insignia. After Kearny first commanded his officers to wear a red patch, and after General Hooker generalized the practice of wearing unit insignia, military commanders are said to have noticed the *esprit de corps* and pride that the insignias brought to the soldiers wearing them. Insignias became a way to show the rest of the world who one was affiliated with—something similar to a sports fan wearing the colors of their home team. To wear insignia is to tell the world that one is a part of something larger than oneself. In the case of a black unit, wearing insignias that identify oneself as a part of a black unit may actually help to preserve whatever secrets the unit may (or may not) hold. By wearing a patch, its wearer advertises to others around him or her that there are certain things that he or she cannot speak about. His or her membership in the secret society is contingent upon keeping those secrets. We might imagine that wearing a patch that speaks to secrets might be extra incentive for the person wearing the patch to keep silent.

Without a doubt, many members of the black world are proud of the secrets they hold, and of the clandestine work they've done in the military or intelligence industries. But others struggle with the alienation that comes along with not being able to tell friends and family what one does for a living and with having a secret life. Obtaining and maintaining a security clearance for black projects can involve federal investigators combing through one's personal life, uncomfortable polygraph examinations, and even surveillance. A few years ago, I talked to a man who had

NELLIS BOMBING AND GUNNERY RANGE

RESTRICTED AREA

NO TRESPASSING
BEYOND THIS POINT

° PHOTOGRAPHY IS PROHIBITED

WARNING

Restricted Area

It is unlawful to enter this area without permission of the Installation Commander.

While on this installation all personnel and the property under their control are subject to search.

Use of deadly force authorized.

The black site at Groom Lake's perimeter is protected by security guards in unmarked trucks.

become frustrated with life in the black world. He didn't like the secrecy, the alienation, the exhaustive and complicated security procedures, and the constant surveillance. He had begun to develop a disdain for his colleagues who seemed to relish that life. When I showed him some of the patches from this book, he was less than enthralled. "I've seen that sort of thing a lot," he said. "Those are gang colors."

ABOUT THIS BOOK

A number of disclaimers are in order. First and foremost, this is not a book of military history, and is not intended to be a comprehensive, historical, or even consistent examination of black world heraldry. Serious collectors of militaria and historians of all varieties may find this book to be maddeningly inconsistent, incomplete—even random. The images contained in these pages are often presented without regard for their unit lineages, and without historical context. To make matters worse for the serious aficionado, I have made no distinction between images scanned from "originals" and those scanned from reproductions. Therefore, the images in this book cannot and should not be relied upon as accurate guides to military history.

Instead, readers of this book will find a collection of images that are fragmentary, torn out of context, inconclusive, unreliable, and deceptive. Readers will find, in other words, a glimpse into the black world itself.

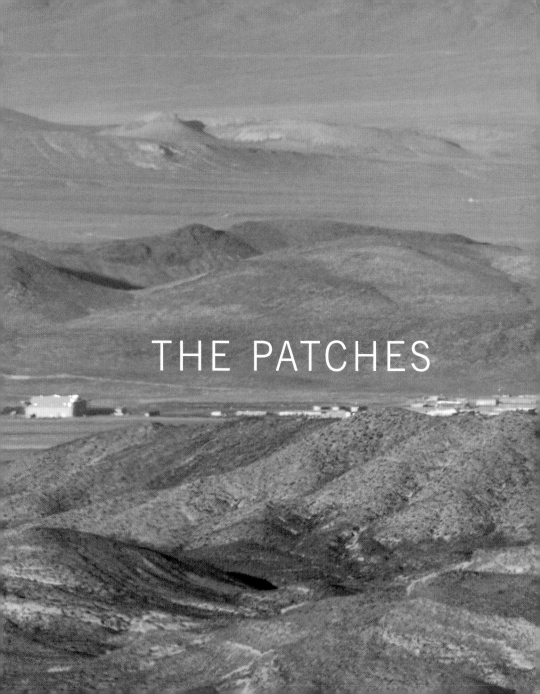

THE PATCHES

SPECIAL PROJECTS FLIGHT
TEST SQUADRON—WIZARD

Based at the Air Force's secret base near Groom Lake, Nevada, the Special Projects Flight Test Squadron is the Air Force's only "black" flight test squadron for classified prototype aircraft and advanced concept technology demonstrators.

The squadron's mascot is a wizard. A collection of six stars $(5+1)$ on the patch references the unit's operating location: the secret base known as Area 51. The lower-case Greek sigma symbol in the wizard's right hand is the engineering symbol for the unknown value of an object's radar cross section (RCS). The ideal radar signature of a stealth aircraft is zero. While no stealth aircraft has yet achieved this goal, several have come close. On the right side of the patch, the falling globe references the hollow aluminum spheres dropped from the sky to calibrate radar equipment. A sphere of a given size has a known RCS value. Lightning bolts, such as the one emanating from the wizard's staff, seem to refer to electronic warfare. The aircraft in the lower right is probably a generic symbol representing flight testing of advanced aircraft. The sword at the bottom of the image refers to a recently declassified Boeing stealth demonstrator known as the "Bird of Prey": the handle on the sword approximates the shape of the aircraft.

SPECIAL PROJECTS FLIGHT
TEST SQUADRON—DIAMOND

An older patch associated with the Special
Projects Flight Test Squadron. The faceted
shape used here may refer to early designs of
stealth aircraft.

RAT 55

"Rat 55" is the call sign used by pilots flying a highly modified T-43A (the Air Force version of a Boeing 737-200) based at a classified air base in central Nevada. The word "Rat" comes from the airplane's function as a Radar Testbed and the "55" comes from the airplane's USAF serial number: 73-1155.

The modified NT-43A is outfitted with radar domes on its nose and tail measuring approximately nine feet long and six and a half feet in diameter and is used to measure the in-flight radar signatures of stealth aircraft.

The NT-43A has been photographed tailing a B-2 stealth bomber over Death Valley and over the Tonopah Test Range in Nevada.

The patch depicts a rat holding a radar in its right hand and another radar dish strapped to its rear-end, both of which recall the radome configuration on the NT-43A. The rat's hat recalls the wizard figures associated with classified flight test operations in other patches.

BIRD OF PREY

The Bird of Prey was a highly classified technology demonstrator that first flew at Groom Lake in 1996. Built by a secretive division of McDonnell Douglas (later acquired by Boeing) known as the "Phantom Works," the aircraft was flown by Boeing pilots Rudy Haug and Joe Felock. Doug Benjamin of the secret Special Projects Flight Test Squadron was the only Air Force pilot to fly the aircraft.

Although the shape of the plane was secret in 1996, the Bird of Prey patch contained an important clue. When Boeing declassified the Bird of Prey's existence in 2002, it became obvious that the handle of the sword was essentially the same shape as the aircraft. This distinctive sword has since become incorporated into the symbolism of the Special Projects Flight Test Squadron.

GHOST SQUADRON

The text on these patches roughly translates as
"A Secret Squadron / From Deep in the Night
/ Don't Ask Any Questions." The patches were
worn by an obscure unit called the "Ghost
Squadron" operating out of the secret Air Force
base near Groom Lake. The single star in the
Southwest United States presumably designates
the group's operating location.

The Ghost Squadron is a helicopter support,
security, and search and rescue team for test
squadrons flying classified aircraft.

G.H.O.S.T.

One of the more recent patches from the "Ghost Squadron" based at Groom Lake. The design of the skull's helmet indicates that "Ghost" is a helicopter unit. The footprints on the helmet mark the trace of the "Jolly Green Giant," a symbol connected to helicopter search and rescue missions. This patch also seems to indicate that "G.H.O.S.T." is an acronym for the unit. The meaning of the acronym is unclear.

PENSER HORS LIMITES

This patch comes from the Operations Group at Groom Lake. The collection of five white stars and one purple star is a reference to Groom Lake's nickname, "Area 51," and here represents the Special Projects Flight Test Squadron. The color purple echoes the colors of other Special Projects Flight Test Squadron patches. The wrench and screwdriver are symbols for aircraft maintenance units and activities. There is also a red star in the bird's eye, which may reference classified squadrons such as the "Red Hats" and "Red Eagles," which were charged with flying purloined Soviet MiGs at the secret base. Green footprints on the cloud symbolize the "Ghost Squadron" search and rescue team. Lightning coming from the cloud spells out the letters "EW" for "electronic warfare" and represents EW test units and activities at the base. The red-and-white and blue-and-white streamers on either side of the bird reference the colors of the Janet planes. (See page 35.)

Penser hors limites is French for "Imagination without boundaries," or "To think beyond the boundaries."

NKAWTG....NOBODY

NKAWTG... NOBODY

This patch comes from an unidentified air
refueling squadron charged with supporting
black aircraft projects. The object in the
character's hand is a fuel boom from a tanker
aircraft such as a KC-135 or a KC-10. The
letters NKAWTG at the bottom of the image
refer to the unofficial motto of the Air Force's
tanker units: "No One Kicks Ass Without
Tanker Gas."

JANET PLANES

The white Boeing 737 with a red stripe
down the fuselage refers to aircraft known as
the "Janet Fleet," because they use the call
sign "Janet" in civilian airspace. The fleet is
operated by the Special Project Division of the
EG&G company; the company's logo provides
the backdrop for the smiling aircraft shown
in the patch. The Janet Fleet shuttles military
and civilian workers to and from their jobs at
secret military bases such as the Tonopah Test
Range and Groom Lake. The Janet Fleet is
headquartered at the "Gold Coast" terminal at
Las Vegas' McCarren Airport.

Workers commute from
Las Vegas to secret
military bases each
morning in unmarked
737s.

A LIFETIME OF SILENCE BEHIND
THE GREEN DOOR

The origins and meaning of this patch are obscure. The green figure holding the sword wears the cloak-and-dagger garb often associated with black projects. There is a white star in the northern hemisphere (under the letter "S") and a red star in the American Southwest.

The patch is likely associated with the Air Force Intelligence, Surveillance and Reconnaissance Agency, based at Lackland Air Force Base in San Antonio, Texas, which perhaps explains the location of the red star. The Air Force ISR Agency's mission is to "Organize, train, equip, and present assigned forces and capabilities to conduct intelligence, surveillance and reconnaissance for combatant commanders and the nation." The agency is involved in a number of "black" projects. The white star in the sky most likely refers to projects involving space capabilities and systems.

The words "A Lifetime of Silence" no doubt refer to the fact that members of this unit or project cannot speak about what they do. Military intelligence officers have a tradition of working behind locked green vault doors, but the symbol is also widely used in popular culture to designate an inaccessible place.

In Mary E. Wilkins-Freeman's 1917 novel *The Green Door*, a young girl named Letitia longs to open a mysterious little green door in her house, but her aunt forbids it with the words "It is not best for you, my dear." The 1956 hit song "Green Door" is about a man who couldn't get into a party raging behind a green door. The 1972 pornographic film *Behind the Green Door* also uses the image to connote an inaccessible place (in the case of the film, a sex theater).

FREEDOMUS AO ANAI COSAMUS

FREEDOMUS AO ANAT COSAMUS

This patch is from an unknown program active at Groom Lake (Area 51) sometime during the late 1990s. The collection of six stars above the eagle's head may represent Area 51 (5 + 1 stars), and the collection of three stars below the eagle might represent "Detachment 3." (Groom Lake is also known as "Air Force Flight Test Center, Detachment 3".) The phrase *Freedomus Ao Anat Cosamus* is a garbled concoction of dog-Latin and dog-Greek. Although the intended meaning of the phrase is unclear, one might venture the guess "Freedom throughout the cosmos."

U.S.A.F. AEROSPACE MEDICINE

AFFTC

BETTER CARE NOWHERE

AEROSPACE MEDICINE

This patch is worn by the aerospace medical personnel assigned to the secret flight test facility at Groom Lake, also known as Air Force Flight Test Center, Detachment 3 (AFFTC Det. 3). Aerospace medicine is a specialized branch of medicine that focuses on the needs of pilots and aircrews.

PANTHER DEN

INFORMATION WARFARE

PANTHER DEN

Panther Den is a Special Access Program (SAP) based at Hanscom Air Force Base in Massachusetts. Managed by the Big Safari project office (pg. 123), Panther Den is charged with overseeing classified information warfare projects. Related to electronic warfare, information warfare involves defending and attacking computer networks and other kinds of information infrastructure.

Projects falling under Panther Den's umbrella include Pirate Sword, Steel Puma, and Project Deborah.

MINOTAUR

Minotaur is a still-classified program
undertaken by Lockheed Martin's Advanced
Development Programs division, the Skunk
Works. Although Minotaur remains obscure,
rumor holds that the airframe shares a
"family resemblance" with another Skunk
Works program called Minion and may have
served as a technology demonstrator for
that program.

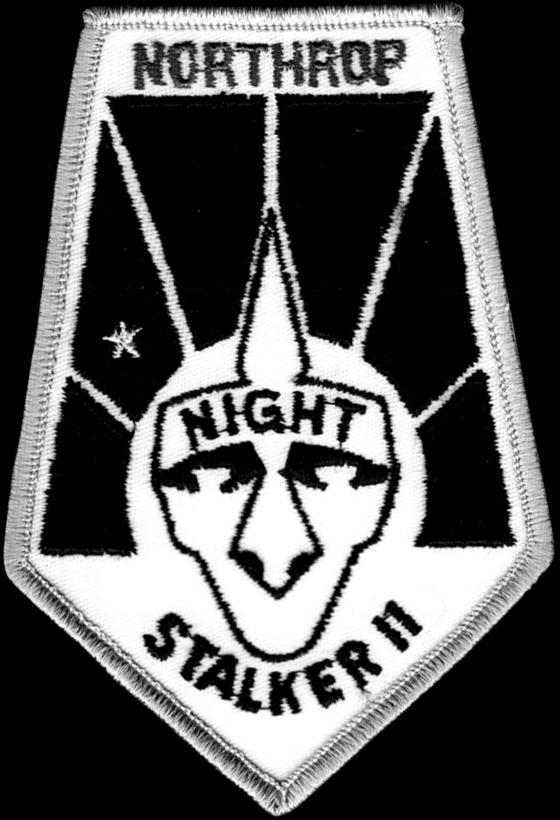
NORTHROP
NIGHT
STALKER II

NORTHROP NIGHT STALKER II

There is no publicly available information about Northrop's "Night Stalker II" program. The numeral II suggests a "Night Stalker I," which remains equally obscure.

SEEKERS FLIGHT TEST

This patch is from the flight test of an unknown aircraft or system conducted by defense contractor Scaled Composites, based near Edwards Air Force Base in Mojave, California.

Scaled Composites became widely known in October of 2004 when the company won the "X-Prize" after launching its "Spaceship One" aircraft to an altitude above 328,000 feet twice in fourteen days.

The company does a significant amount of classified work for the Department of Defense. Job listings on Scaled Composites' web site indicate that the company prefers to hire workers in possession of a "DOD Secret Clearance."

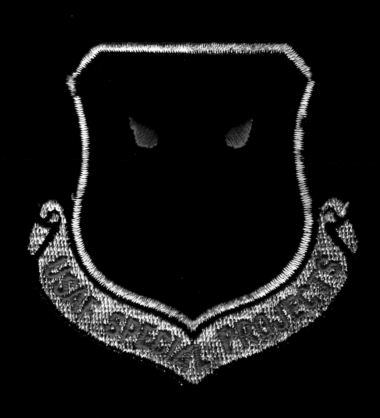

USAF SPECIAL PROJECTS

This unofficial patch was created by the
46th Test Wing, Eglin Air Force Base, in
commemoration of multiple Electronic
Warfare development programs. When
primary responsibility for USAF EW testing
was transferred from Eglin to Edwards Air
Force Base as part of the Base Realignment
and Closure process, the patch also moved
to Edwards and became associated with
the 413th Flight Test Squadron. While the
413th at Edwards was decommissioned
in 2004, the patch is still in use at various
locations, presumably in support of new EW
capabilities.

Alone and Unafraid

ALONE AND UNAFRAID

This is one of several patches associated with the Lockheed Martin "Desert Prowler" program, an Unmanned Aerial Vehicle (UAV) first flown on December 13, 2005. The numerals 9 and 11 also appear on other patches associated with the program. The collection of 5 + 1 stars in the lower left section of the patch refers to the classified flight test center at Groom Lake, suggesting that the UAV underwent flight test at the black site or was tested at another site (such as Lockheed's "Area 6" near Yucca Lake) with support from Groom Lake units.

Desert Prowler may be related to a classified UAV operating out of Kandahar, Afghanistan, that began operations around 2007. Aviation journalist Bill Sweetman initially dubbed the aircraft "the Beast of Kandahar" after a French magazine published a blurry image of the unknown vehicle. On December 4, 2009, the Air Force confirmed the existence of an aircraft called the RQ-170 Sentinel. The RQ-170 is operated by the 30th Reconnaissance Squadron based at the Tonopah Test Range in Nevada.

IX   XI

ALONE AND ON THE PROWL

ALONE AND ON THE PROWL

Another patch associated with the Lockheed
Martin Unmanned Aerial Vehicle first flown
in late 2005.

DESERT PROWLER

Yet another patch associated with Lockheed Martin's "Desert Prowler" program.

The figure here is taken from the cover art of the hip-hop duo Insane Clown Posse's sixth "joker card" album, entitled *The Wraith: Shangri-La*. In the narrative of the concept album, the Wraith takes the listener on a tour through heaven and hell.

SNEEKY PETE

Another patch from an obscure Scaled
Composites project; the symbolism is unclear.
The name Pete may refer to Scaled Composites
test pilot Peter Siebold.

Marines sometimes refer to reconnaissance
missions as "Sneeky Pete" work, as in, "We're
going Sneeky Pete."

GLOBAL ENGAGEMENT MILITARY SPACEPLANE

This patch is from the Phillips Laboratory Military Spaceplane Technology (MiST) Program Office at Kirtland Air Force Base in New Mexico.

The original version of the patch sported an "X-Wing" fighter from the *Star Wars* movies. When lawyers representing George Lucas delivered the unit a cease and desist order, the aircraft on the patch was changed to the shape that appears on this patch.

SPACE WARFARE CENTER
SPECIAL PROJECTS DIVISION

Based at Schriever Air Force Base in Colorado, the Space Warfare Center's mission is to evaluate the performance of space and missile systems, integrate space systems into military operations, and train space systems operators.

The Special Projects Division presumably performs similar functions for "black" space systems.

IF I TELL YOU I
HAVE TO KILL YOU

A generic patch for "black" projects designed
by a member of Air Test and Evaluation
Squadron Four (VX-4), based at Point Mugu
near Camarillo, California. VX-4 eventually
merged with VX-5 from NAWC China Lake, also
in Southern California, to become VX-9 with
detachments at both locations.

TRIANGULUM

"Triangulum" is reported to designate a
variation on the RS6b SENIOR SPEAR sensor
system built into some versions of the U-2 spy
plane. The Triangulum system allegedly uses
twelve antennae along the aircraft's fuselage
and an antenna on each wing.

VINDICATOR

Built by Lockheed Martin's Skunk Works, the
Vindicator system was a highly classified project
(rumored to be "more secret than the F-117A,"
the stealth fighter program) from the 1980s.
This patch includes the Lockheed Advanced
Development Projects' skunk mascot wearing
a helmet and scarf. The patch depicts a laser
anemometer optical air data system, which takes
the place of conventional pitot-static probes on
stealth or high-speed aircraft where physical
protrusions are undesirable. The device is
a velocity indicator (or, in aviation parlance,
a *v*-indicator).

L.O. FLIGHT TEST

HUGE DEPOSIT -- NO RETURN

LO FLIGHT TEST

The words "LO Flight Test" describe a "Low
Observables" flight test, in all probability a radar
measurement test for a stealth aircraft using
the radar measurement range at Groom Lake,
Nevada. The date of this particular flight test
is unknown, but the test reportedly involved a
B-2 stealth bomber. The sigma symbol in the
middle of the patch refers to the unknown value
of the aircraft's radar cross section (sigma/zero
being the ideal radar cross section measurement
for a stealth plane). "Huge deposit" indicates
the bomb load deposited by the bomber on its
target, while "no return" refers to the absence
of a radar-return, meaning that the aircraft was
undetectable to radar. It is unclear why there
is a star on the tail of the sigma, though it may
simply be an artistic touch.

RED HATS — MORE WITH LESS

Red Hats was a nickname for the 6513th Test Squadron, which was charged with testing a collection of Soviet military aircraft surreptitiously acquired from foreign sources. The 6513th was based at Groom Lake, Nevada, in a collection of hangars on the northern end of the base that became known as "Red Square." The program to test Soviet MiGs at Groom Lake began in the late 1960s as a joint CIA/USAF effort under the code names HAVE DRILL and HAVE DOUGHNUT.

Again, note the collection of six stars on the patch, which may refer to Groom Lake's nickname, Area 51.

The 6513th was deactivated in 1992 and transformed into the 413th Flight Test Squadron.

413th FLIGHT
TEST SQUADRON

The 413th Test Squadron was designated and activated on October 2, 1992, when it was formed out of the disbanded 6513th Red Hats Test Squadron. The Red Hats had conducted flight testing of purloined Soviet MiGs and other aircraft at Groom Lake. In March 1994, the unit became the 413th Flight Test Squadron, nicknamed the "Bombcats."

Based at a restricted section of Edwards Air Force Base called "North Base," the mission of the 413th was to organize flight tests of Electronic Warfare systems around the world. A detachment of the 413th, called the "Nutcrackers," continued to operate out of Groom Lake and the Tonopah Test Range. Daily flights in unmarked Beech aircraft shuttled members of the 413th to the secret bases each day.

The 413th was responsible for a number of programs; code names included SUNDOWNER, ZIPPER, and IBIS DAWN. In May of 2004, the squadron was deactivated (although the unit designation was later transferred to a squadron formed from a detachment of the 46th Operations Group at Eglin Air Force Base in Florida). The remaining "Bombcats" assets became part of the Electronic Warfare Directorate, also headquartered at Edwards Air Force Base.

PROJECT ZIPPER

This patch represents an unknown project
undertaken by the 413th Flight Test Squadron.
The zipper seems to refer to the fact that the
project cannot be discussed. The first part of
the phrase "We make threats" might refer to
making simulated (or real) electronic "threats"
against aircraft.

NUTCRACKERS

"Nutcrackers" was an alter ego of the 413th
Flight Test Squadron referring to detachments
operating at classified locations that included
Groom Lake and the Tonopah Test Range.

The collection of 4+1+3 stars on the left side
of the patch refers to the 413th Flight Test
Squadron. The crow and the lightning bolts
symbolize the unit's electronic warfare mission.

EW DIRECTORATE

The Electronic Warfare Directorate is the primary EW test organization at Edwards Air Force Base.

Electronic warfare consists of defensive and offensive avionics and includes the so-called "Infowar" revolution in military technologies. Commenting on information warfare, Air Force Chief of Staff John Jumper told *Aviation Week and Space Technology* that "we're rapidly approaching the time when you can tell an SA-10's [surface-to-air missile system] radar that it's a Maytag washer and put it in the rinse cycle instead of the firing cycle."

EWAH

This patch is worn by personnel working for a unit descended from the 413th Flight Test Squadron. Elements of the former 413th FLTS became a part of the EW Directorate known by its organization code EWAH. Located at North Base at Edwards, EWAH has its own commanding officer who reports directly to the EW Directorate.

The collection of 5 + 1 stars recalls the nickname Area 51, the Air Force's classified "operating location" at Groom Lake.

Opposite:
A symbol on the inside of the plane's cockpit shows a collection of five-plus-one stars.

Above:
Nicknamed "the Whale," Northrop's TACIT BLUE was an early stealth technology demonstrator. It first flew at Groom Lake in 1982 and was retired in 1985. The Air Force made the existence of the black aircraft public in 1996.

Both images: USAF

KILLER WHALE

"Killer Whale" was a nickname for the AGM-137 Tri-Service Standoff Attack Missile, also known as TSSAM, which was a project to develop a stealth cruise missile during the 1980s. The name "Killer Whale" has a somewhat complicated history. In the early 1980s, Northrop developed a stealthy prototype aircraft codenamed "TACIT BLUE," which pioneered the use of rounded shapes for stealth aircraft. Because of the plane's unusual shape, it became known as the "Whale" or "Shamu," and the Northrop crews working on the project at Groom Lake became known as "whalers." After TACIT BLUE, which was unarmed, proved that this stealth technology was effective, Northrop began work on the Tri-Service Standoff Attack Missile, which was a variation on the TACIT BLUE design, and resembled the unusually-shaped stealth aircraft. Thus, while the unarmed TACIT BLUE was known as the "Whale," its cruise missile cousin became known as the "Killer Whale."

The Latin phrase *"Deterritum Per Testandum Supra Terram"* is hard to decipher. The words vaguely translate as "Deterrence/Through/Witness/Above/Earth." Members of the test team choose to interpret it loosely as "Deterrence Through Flight Test."

TSSAM

Because the acronym for the Tri-Service Standoff
Attack Missile (TSSAM) recalled the "Tasmanian
Devil" cartoon character, the tornado-like image
of the character in motion came to represent the
classified cruise missile.

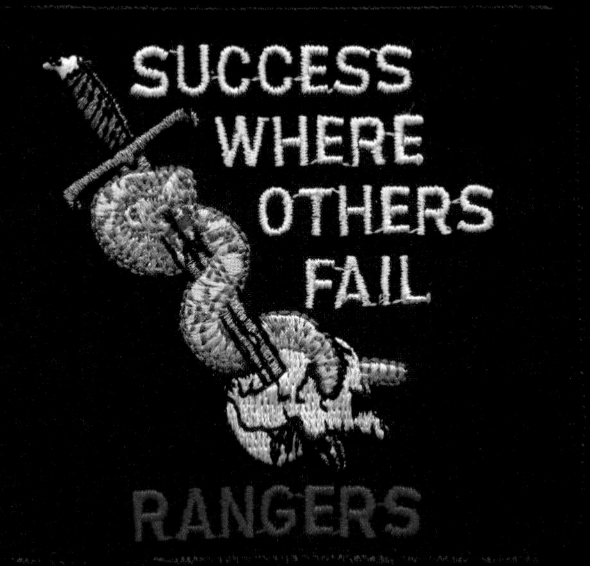
SUCCESS
WHERE
OTHERS
FAIL
RANGERS

RANGERS

This patch was designed by security personnel (know as "Rangers") assigned to classified locations within the Air Force's Nellis Range Complex.

The design was inspired, in part, by popular stories about ninjas patrolling Nellis black sites. USAF security personnel, whose training and job duties are rather pedestrian, began wearing this patch as an ironic response.

RANGE PATCH

This patch represents various classified locations
within the Air Force's Nellis Range Complex in
the Nevada desert.

The meaning of these symbols is unknown.

4477th TEST & EVALUATION SQUADRON — "RED EAGLES"

From its inception in 1975, the 4477th Test and Evaluation Squadron conducted tactical evaluations of a highly classified squadron of Soviet fighters in U.S. possession.

The unit was based at Groom Lake until the late 1970s and early 1980s, when the 4477th provided $24 million towards the initial construction of another classified operating location in Central Nevada: the Tonopah Test Range, also known as Area 52.

The 4477th seems to have been disbanded sometime in the early 1990s and its mission taken over by Detachment 2 of the 57th Fighter Wing. Eventually, this became Detachment 3 of the 53rd Test and Evaluation Group.

DET-2 57TH WING

DET-3 53RD TEG

57th FIGHTER WING, DETACHMENT 2

Although all activities associated with Detachment 2 of the 57th Fighter Wing remain classified, it is known that the unit operates under the Advanced Programs office of the 57th Wing. According to official documents from the 57th Wing, which is based at Nellis Air Force Base in Las Vegas, Detachment 2 "operates off-location to support tactical development for the combat air forces."

DET 2, 57 FW (now DET 3, 53 TEG) has probably taken over much of the 4477th "Red Eagles" mission to provide tactical evaluation of foreign aircraft. Its "off-location" operating base is most likely Groom Lake (Area 51) or the Tonopah Test Range (Area 52).

SEMPER EN OBSCURUS

This patch comes from the Special Projects
Office, which operated out of the Air Force's
Sacramento Air Logistics Center and oversaw
maintenance and support of the F-117A
stealth fighter program. The phrase "*Semper en
Obscurus*" translates as "Always in the Dark."
The mushroom—which grows in darkness—
symbolizes the secret nature of the Office's work.
This same patch is now used by the 412th
Test Wing's Special Projects Office at Edwards
Air Force Base.

RAPID CAPABILITIES OFFICE

Among other things, the Rapid Capabilities Office at Air Force headquarters in Washington is responsible for technical integration of the Department of Defense's classified activities, and for reporting these activities to the Air Force leadership, the office of the secretary of defense, Congress, and the White House.

The symbol in the background of this patch is a black and gray image of the earth, representing the "black world" of classified activities. The Latin at the bottom of the patch translates as "Doing God's work with other people's money."

DIRECTORATE OF
SPECIAL PROJECTS

The Directorate of Special Projects works
with the Office of the Secretary of Defense
and Congress to direct financial oversight,
programmatic evaluation, budget formulation
and acquisition management of the $2.2
billion annual Air Force special access program
portfolio. The image on the patch recalls a
classified aircraft flying above a "black world."

PETE'S DRAGON II

When, in July of 1982, pilot Pete Barnes
was scheduled for his first flight in the still-
secret stealth fighter, he found that the plane
had a green dragon painted on the side. The
inspiration for the design came from the Disney
film *Pete's Dragon*, which was about a green
dragon named Elliot who was invisible
to everyone except a boy named Pete.

A few years later, Pete Barnes took control of
an upgraded stealth fighter, commemorated by
the patch shown here. Pete's Dragon eventually
morphed into the "Dragon Test Team."

DON'T ASK — NOYFB

This patch is from the 22nd Military Airlift
Squadron, which flew C-5 cargo aircraft out of
Travis Air Force Base in Northern California. Part
of the 22nd MAS' mission was to conduct late
night operations picking up classified aircraft
from aerospace plants in Southern California and
delivering them to classified locations for testing
and evaluation.

When the 22nd MAS undertook these missions,
its crews would take off their everyday heraldry
and Velcro this patch to their uniforms.

The black background and crescent moon on
the patch probably represent the unit's night
operations. The silver lining represents star light.
The letters "NOYFB" stand for "None of Your
Fucking Business."

GOAT SUCKERS

Goat Suckers designates the Q-Unit of the
4452nd Test Squadron, charged in the early
1980s with testing and evaluating a growing
squadron of top-secret stealth fighters at the
Tonopah Test Range.

In addition to the stealth fighters, the Goat
Suckers flew a collection of A-7 Corsair fighters,
which were used as chase planes and proficiency
trainers. The A-7 also became a cover story for
the stealth fighter when its existence was still
classified. When stealth pilots were asked about
the 4452nd Test Squadron, they would claim
that they flew A-7s.

The name Goatsuckers refers to a family of
nocturnal birds that, folklore held, fed on goat's
milk at night. Included in the Goatsucker family
of birds is *chordeiles minor*: the Nighthawk.

Nighthawk is the nickname of the F-117A stealth
fighter; the existence of the F-117A was classified
until November 8, 1988.

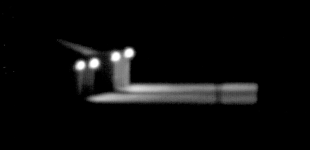

The Tonopah Test
Range at night.

F3XP M.A.R.S.

During the years when the F-117A stealth fighter
was a black project operating out of the Tonopah
Test Range, a secret program known only by the
code name F3XP was designed to repair and
maintain the aircraft's radar absorbent coatings.
Composed of Air Force corrosion control specialists
and sheet metal technicians, members of this
project, called the Materials Application Repair
Section (M.A.R.S.), were known as "Martians."

GRIM REAPERS

GRIM REAPERS

Grim Reapers was the nickname of the 4451st Test Squadron, which operated under the 4450th Tactical Group at the Tonopah Test Range during the 1980s. The unit's mission was to fly a squadron of classified stealth fighters.

When the Pentagon announced the existence of the stealth fighter program in the late 1980s, the Grim Reapers were redesignated as the 416th Tactical Fighter Squadron. After the Grim Reapers' existence became public, the Air Force forced the unit to change their name, as it did not pass the Air Force's requirements for good taste. The Grim Reapers thus became the Ghost Riders.

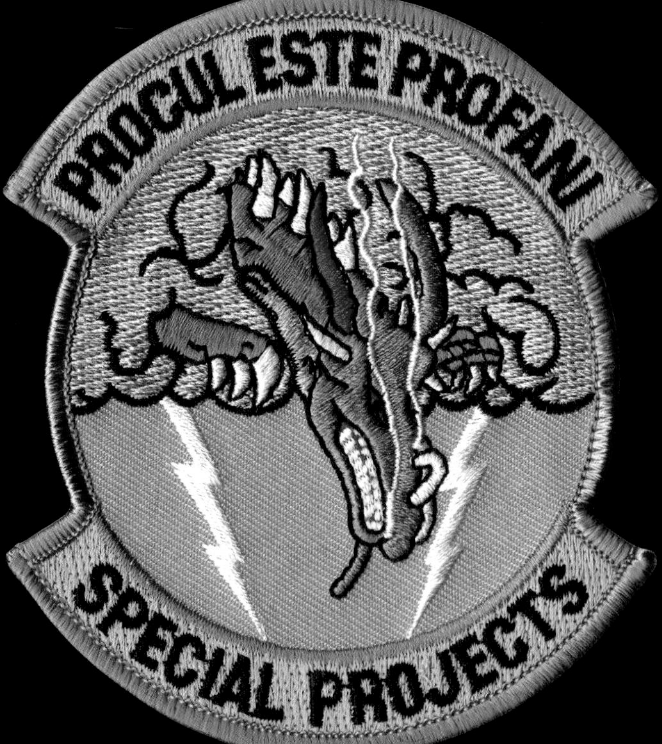
PROCUL ESTE PROFANI
SPECIAL PROJECTS

PROCUL ESTE PROFANI —
SPECIAL PROJECTS

This patch is from the 416th Flight Test
Squadron's Special Projects Flight working on
advanced technologies for the F-16 Combined
Test Force at Edwards Air Force Base.

The phrase *Procul Este Profani* is usually
associated with Virgil's epic poem *The Aeneid*.
When Apollo arrives at the Temple of Apollo,
the prophet Sibyl utters the words *"Procul,
O procul este profane"* before the pair descend
into Hades, where Aeneas is told about the
future of Rome.

Members of the unit translate the phrase as
"Keep your distance, you who are uninitiated."

CLASSIFIED FLIGHT TEST

GUSTATUS SIMILIS PULLUS

509

TO SERVE MAN

GUSTATUS SIMILIS PULLUS

509

CLASSIFIED FLIGHT TEST

This was the original version of a patch commemorating a flight test series involving a B-2 "Spirit" stealth bomber. The Greek sigma symbol on the test shape's outline signifies the unknown RCS value. The number "509" refers to the 509th Bomb Wing, which operates the United States' stealth bombers from Whiteman Air Force Base in Missouri. The alien is a reference to the 509th's infamous lineage. In 1947, the 509th was based at Roswell, New Mexico, home of the "Roswell incident," which ensued after the 509th's commander, Col. William Blanchard, issued a press release with the headline "Roswell Army Airfield Captures Flying Saucer on Ranch in Roswell Region."

The dog-Latin phrase *Gustasus Similis Pullus* translates as "Tastes Like Chicken." Note the knife and fork.

This patch was eventually modified when Air Force officials insisted that the phrase "Classified Flight Test" not appear on the design. In an updated version of the patch, "Classified Flight Test" has been replaced with the words "To Serve Man," referencing a classic episode of *The Twilight Zone*.

BIG SAFARI

Big Safari is the code name for a program office at the Air Force Material Command at Wright Patterson Air Force Base in Ohio. Founded in 1953, the code name "Big Safari" was classified for decades.

Big Safari is responsible for aircraft specifically designed or modified for missions, including a fleet of RC-135 spy planes codenamed RIVET JOINT.

This patch is from the years when the name Big Safari was classified. The lightning bolts probably refer to electronic warfare. The hog almost certainly refers to RC-135 aircraft, which are sometimes called "hogs" because of their extended noses. The cobra may refer to the code name COBRA BALL, which is the code name for a variation of the RC-135. The dog sniffing the man's foot may refer to the code name COMFY HOUND, which was a quarterly report of electronic warfare activities.

BIG SAFARI PROGRAM

When the code name Big Safari became declassified, the name began to appear on the patch worn by members of the Big Safari Program Office.

Recent projects developed under the Big Safari Program Office include COMPASS CALL (an EC-130H electronic warfare platform), RIVET RIDER (an airborne television broadcast station), PANTHER DEN (an information warfare program office at Hanscom Air Force Base), SCATHE MEAN (a project using decoy drones in the first Gulf War), DISTANT PHOENIX (probably an air-sampling program over the Pacific Ocean in the mid-1990s), and SCATHE VIEW (a program using video cameras embedded in conventional aircraft as a hidden reconnaissance platform).

NATIONAL RECONNAISSANCE OFFICE

WE OWN THE NIGHT

2000

NATIONAL RECONNAISSANCE OFFICE
"WE OWN THE NIGHT"

This patch commemorates the August 17, 2000, launch of a "classified National Reconnaissance Office payload" atop a Titan IV rocket from Vandenberg Air Force Base in Southern California.

Clues in the patch's imagery seem to indicate that the satellite in question was, in fact, an ONYX spy satellite, also known by the code name Lacrosse. The owl eyes and the phrase "We Own the Night" seem to imply an imaging platform that can "see" in darkness, indicating a satellite that uses synthetic aperture radar to produce images of the Earth's surface. The wire mesh surrounding the owl's eyes is perhaps indicative of the mesh on ONYX satellites, which is purported to cover its antennae.

The triangular images on the patch represent other ONYX satellites, all of which are in a reconnaissance orbit. (Different satellite orbits do different "jobs.") Two of the filled-in shapes represent active ONYX satellites. The hollowed-out shape represents "Lacrosse I," which was de-orbited in 1997 after nine years in service (it was originally deployed from the space shuttle Atlantis on mission STS-27). The third solid shape represents the satellite being launched.

ALIEN TECHNOLOGY
EXPLOITATION DIVISION

The Alien Technology Exploitation Division patch was designed by Robert Fabian during the time he was assigned to a classified unit working in a secure facility at Air Force Space command:

> I designed this patch several years ago while stationed at Headquarters, Air Force Space Command. A couple of friends and I pooled our money and had them made—strictly unofficially. I'm afraid there's not a whole lot of symbolism in it. We were working inside a SCIF (vault) and our friends and coworkers used to like giving us a hard time about it, asking if our office was where they kept the alien bodies. As a joke, we told them that dead aliens were no use; we needed live ones to explain their technology to us. After one particularly grueling late night working on briefing slides that went nowhere, we came up with the patch idea. The Klingon translates to "Don't Ask!"

> We wore them on our flightsuits for a couple of months before anyone in authority spotted them. Our boss's boss's boss, a Brigadier General, only reaction was to ask where he could get one.

CATCH A FALLING STAR

Between the launch of the first photo-
reconnaissance satellite in 1960 and the
maturation of digital imaging chips in the 1970s,
spy satellites produced photographs on long
sheets of film. After the satellite's camera had
exposed a roll, the film canister ejected from the
spacecraft and parachuted towards Earth. Special
film-recovery teams were charged with catching
the film canisters midair over the Pacific using
specially modified aircraft based in Hawaii. This
patch was worn by the 6594th Test Group, which
was charged with these sensitive missions.

PAN

PAN is a classified spacecraft launched into a geostationary orbit from Cape Canaveral on September 8, 2009. PAN is unique among classified American satellites because, while it is discussed by contractors and appears on military launch schedules, it is not publicly "claimed" by any intelligence or military agency. Space analysts have speculated that the Central Intelligence Agency may be responsible for the satellite.

While some analysts believe the acronym PAN stands for "Pick a Name," the launch patch for PAN contains the phrase "Palladium at Night." In Greek and Roman mythology, a palladium was a sacred object—like a statue—that was believed to protect the city or state possessing it. "Pan" could also refer to the Greek god known for inspiring fear and confusion ("pan" is the root of "panic"). PAN may act as a communications relay for armed CIA Predator and Reaper drones operating in Pakistan and Afghanistan.

SENSOR HUNTER

The unit associated with the Sensor Hunter patch
is unknown. Based on the symbolism, it seems
likely that it is devoted to reconnaissance and
intelligence operations.

UHF F/O

The U.S. Navy's Ultra High Frequency Follow On (UFO) program is a series of communications satellites designed to replace older Fleet Satellite Communications (FLTSATCOM) and Leasat spacecraft.

The Navy uses UFO satellites as a global communications network, connecting ships at sea, fixed installations, and mobile terminals.

The first UFO satellite (Block 1) was launched in 1993, and the most recent UFO (Block 4) was launched in 2003.

UNKNOWN DRAGON PATCH

The program associated with this patch remains obscure, but its symbolism provides a number of clues. Overall, the patch strongly suggests a signal intelligence (SIGINT) spacecraft. Dragons have long been associated with SIGINT launches, and the dragon's wings underline the connection (golden dragon wings often symbolize the massive gold-foil dish antennae characteristic of SIGINT spacecraft). Moreover, the red arrow's trajectory suggests a Molniya orbit similar to the JUMPSEAT and TRUMPET spacecraft. In the visual language of classified space launch patches, stars often represent the number of spacecraft in a given lineage or "constellation." The stars here suggest that this spacecraft is being added to a preexisting constellation of five other craft with similar missions.

The meanings of the red point in Asia and the snake-like figure in the lower part of the patch are unclear, although the cobra may refer to a "COBRA"-series sensor platform related to other SIGINT technologies such as "COBRA BRASS," "COBRA BALL," and "COBRA JUDY."

The Latin phrase *Omnis Vestri Substructio Es Servus Ad Nobis* recalls a 2001–2002 internet meme from a poorly translated Japanese video game: "All Your Base Are Belong to Us." In the opening dialog of the game, an operator says, "We get signal."

NITWITS RUBES OAFS, SETEC ASTRONOMY

The first letter of each word in the phrase
"Nitwits Rubes and Oafs" spells out the agency
responsible for this patch: the NRO, the National
Reconnaissance Office. Furthermore, "OAFS"
could be an acronym for Onizuka Air Force
Station, an Air Force Space Operations base in
Sunnyvale, California, colloquially known as
the Blue Cube.

It is unclear what the collection of three white
stars and one black star represents, although
these may be related to the collection of four
triangles from the NRO's "We Own the Night"
patch depicted on pg. 127.

The phrase "Setec Astronomy" figures prominently
in the 1992 film *Sneakers*, in which the phrase
is an anagram for "Too Many Secrets."

OD-4 / DL AND DX

These patches are from Operating Division 4
of the National Reconnaissance Office. In the
OD-4 / DX patch, the phrase "We Own the Night"
recalls the phrase associated with the radar-
imaging capabilities on the ONYX series of spy
satellites. The figure of the owl is also consistent
with the theme of seeing at night. The mesh-
like structure seems to represent the imaging
capabilities of reconnaissance satellites in general,
while the polar orbits represented by the rings
around the globe are consistent with the types of
orbits used by spy satellites.

MISSION OPERATIONS—
YOU CAN RUN...

Another patch associated with Operating Division 4 of the National Reconnaissance Office. The background pattern of stars seems to represent the night sky, with the single white star signifying a reconnaissance satellite. Three orbits are depicted around the Earth, all of which are associated with different reconnaissance tasks.

The horizontal orbit around the Earth represents a geostationary orbit for communications and (in the case of the NRO) signals intelligence collection. The Rhyolite/Aquacade series of satellites, for example, were kept in a geostationary orbit over Indochina to constantly monitor Soviet and Chinese communications during the Cold War. The downlink for the Rhyolite satellites was located in the Australian outback at Pine Gap, where the collected signals were encrypted, then sent to the NSA at Fort Meade via another geosynchronous satellite.

The highly elliptical ring depicted on the patch represents a Molniya orbit, which allows a reconnaissance satellite to spend most of its time over one particular region of the Earth and is often used by SIGINT satellites.

The third ring represents a polar orbit, an orbit often associated with imaging and photography because a satellite in such an orbit will cover much larger swaths of the Earth's surface than satellites in other orbits.

AF TENCAP SPECIAL APPLICATIONS

TENCAP is an acronym for Tactical Exploitation of National Capabilities, a collection of programs that involve developing tactical (battlefield) applications out of reconnaissance satellite capabilities (which are normally thought of as strategic).

"Special" almost invariably means "black" or highly classified.

The phrase *"Oderint Dum Metuant"* is associated with Caligula, the First century Roman emperor whose name became synonymous with depravity, madness, cruelty, and tyranny. It translates "Let them hate so long as they fear."

Numquam Ante Numquam Iterum

NRO — SNAKES

This patch was designed for the November 8, 1997, launch of spacecraft USA-136, which is believed to be the third spacecraft in the TRUMPET constellation (also known as JEROBOAM). The TRUMPET constellation consists of three spacecraft: USA-103, USA-112, and USA-136.

The three snakes probably represent the three spacecraft that make up TRUMPET, and the three stars at the top of the patch may refer to the same. The way the snakes encircle the earth may also be significant: two of the tails seem to illustrate highly inclined molniya-type orbits, designed to loiter over northern latitudes, while the third seems to illustrate a geostationary orbit. This is curious because all three TRUMPET spacecraft are known to have been placed in molniya orbits.

The Latin inscription reads "Never Before Never Again."

In documents submitted to the United Nations in compliance with the Convention on Objects Launched into Space, the United States described USA-136 as a "spacecraft engaged in practical applications and uses of space technology such as weather or communications."

NRO — DRAGON

This is a program patch from the National Reconnaissance Office, the United States' "black" space agency whose existence was a secret until the early 1990s (the agency was formed in the early 1960s).

The patch is associated with a classified satellite launched into geosynchronous orbit from Cape Canaveral on September 9, 2003. Known by the code names MENTOR and ADVANCED ORION, the spacecraft is a late-generation signals-intelligence satellite descended from the 1970s–era RHYOLITE program.

In a series of 2008 articles in *The Space Review*, Dwayne Day showed that the dragon figure has been associated with space-based SIGINT platforms going back as far as the 1970s. Large, outspread wings are associated with SIGINT spacecraft and thought to represent the circular, football-field sized antennas used to collect stray signals from earth.

The meaning of the diamond is unknown.

MELIOR

This patch for National Reconnaissance Office Launch 49 shows a phoenix rising from flames, with fourteen stars in the background, another star obscured by the bird's wing, along with the Latin phrase "melior diabolus quem scies."

Dwane Day, writing in *The Space Review*, has argued that the fourteen stars represent the number of satellites in the KH-11 electro-optical reconnaissance family since its debut in 1976, and that the obscured star signifies a failed launch.

The KH-11 series was supposed to be replaced by a twenty-first century system called Future Imagery Architecture (FIA). The FIA program, however, was cancelled after massive budget overruns and technology failures. In the meantime, the NRO was left with a shrinking constellation of active KH-11s (there are usually four KH-11s in orbit at one time).

The patch for NROL-49 strongly suggests that it will be a final one for the KH-11; the launch is said to have been assembled from spare parts. Thus, the symbolism of a bird rising from fire and ash may represent a KH-11 rising from FIA's demise.

The Latin phrase seems to strongly corroborate this. *"Melior diabolus quem scies,"* translates as "Better the devil you know."

SI EGO CERTIOREM

This patch was designed as a generic insignia for "black" projects conducted by the Navy's Air Test and Evaluation Squadron Four (VX-4) based at Point Mugu, California. It was reportedly used during the navy's involvement with the TSSAM program. It may still be worn by members of the VX-9 squadron formed from a merger of VX-4 and VX-5. VX-9's mission is to test strike aircraft, conventional weapons, electronic warfare equipment, and to develop tactics involving these weapons systems. The Latin phrase "*Si Ego Certiorem Faciam… Mihi Tu Delendus Eris*" roughly translates into a cliché commonly heard in the vicinity of "black" programs: "I could tell you, but then I'd have to kill you."

But the phrasing here is unusual because it is written in the passive voice: a more accurate translation of the Latin would be "I could tell you, but then you would have to be destroyed by me." By employing the passive voice the patch's designer makes two references that don't exist in other phrasings. The first reference is to the Greek God of Chaos, Eris, about whom Homer wrote in Book Four of the *Iliad*:

"[Eris] whose wrath is relentless, she is the sister and companion of murderous Ares. She who is only a little thing at the first, but thereafter grows until she strides on the earth with her head striking heaven. She then hurled down bitterness equally between both sides as she walked through the onslaught making men's pain heavier."

The passive phrasing of the Latin also echoes the words of Second century B.C. Roman senator Cato the Elder, who roamed the Senate repeating the words "*Carthago delenda est*"—"Carthage must be destroyed." In 149 B.C., Cato got his wish and Rome attacked the city, which was located in North Africa near present-day Tunis. Three years after beginning their assault, the Roman army overran Carthage, tore down its walls, and sold its inhabitants into slavery. After the Roman Senate declared that no one would ever live where Carthage had stood, legend holds that Rome salted the earth around the city in order to ensure that Carthage would remain a wasteland for generations.

ACKNOWLEDGEMENTS

Although this book's title page bears the name of a single author, projects such as this are by their very nature collaborative endeavors. The book you're holding is no exception. Numerous people have given me generous access to their time, insight, and to their personal collections in order to realize this project. The majority of them, for obvious reasons, wish to remain anonymous. You know who you are. I thank you immensely. For the record, I'd like to acknowledge the contributions of Peter Merlin, Bugs Mitchell, T. Glen Larson, Rebecca Zorach, Iain Boal and the folks from Dreamland Resort for helping me find and understand the images that have gone into this collection.

I'd also like to thank my colleagues in academia and the arts for their consistent inspiration and support: Negar Azimi, *Bidoun* magazine, Colby Chamberlain, *Cabinet* magazine, Lauren Cornell, Beatriz da Costa, Apsara DiQuinzio, Eyebeam Art and Technology Center, Lisa Farjam, Aaron Gach and CTM, Ruth Wilson Gilmore, Ken Goldberg, Renée Green, Gillian Hart, IAA, Adriene Jenik, Thomas Keenan, Shiloh Krupar, Laura Kurgan, Jean Lave, Simon Leung, Michael Light, Yates McKee, Julia Meltzer, Lize Mogel, Sina Najafi, Greg Niemeyer, Marisa Olson, Jack Paglen, Allan and Michele Pred, Rhizome.org, Ananya Roy, Rebecca Solnit, Liz Thomas, A. C. Thompson, Nato Thompson, David Thorne, Anne Walsh, Michael Watts, and Benjamin Young. Praba Pilar belongs in a class of her own.

I'm eternally grateful to Becky Smith, Kristina Ernst, Greg Hopkins, Bellwether Gallery, and Ted Weinstein. They make this and other work possible. Above all, I'd like to thank Kelly Burdick and Melville House for their commitment to this rather unusual project.

Trevor Paglen is an artist, writer, and geographer. He is the author of *Torture Taxi: On the Trail of the CIA's Rendition Flights* (co-authored with A.C. Thompson), *Blank Spots on a Map: The Dark Geography of the Pentagon's Secret World*, and *Invisible: Covert Operations and Classified Landscapes*. He lives and works in Oakland and New York City.

I Could Tell You But Then You Would Have to Be Destroyed by Me
Emblems from the Pentagon's Black World

© 2008, 2010 Trevor Paglen

First Melville House Paperback Printing: November 2010

Interior Design: Carol Hayes

Melville House Publishing
145 Plymouth Street
Brooklyn, NY 11201
mhpbooks.com

ISBN: 978-1-935554-14-1

Printed in China

Library of Congress Control Number: 2010932520